THIS IS A WELBECK CHILDREN'S BOOK
Published in 2020 by Welbeck Children's Books Limited
An imprint of the Welbeck Publishing Group
20 Mortimer Street, London W1T 3JW
Text, design and illustration © Welbeck Publishing Limited 2020
ISBN: 978-1-78312-534-0

Writer: Simon Mugford
Designer and Illustrator: Dan Green
Design manager: Emily Clarke
Editorial manager: Joff Brown
Production: Nicola Davey

A catalogue record for this book is available from the British Library.

Printed in the UK
10 9 8 7 6 5 4 3 2 1

Statistics and records correct as of October 2019

FOOTBALL SUPERSTARS

MESSI

RULES

SIMON MUGFORD   DAN GREEN

CONTENTS

MESSI!, MESSI! MESSI!

Is **Lionel Messi** the best footballer in the world? You are reading this book because you think he is **BRILLIANT, AMAZING** and the **GREATEST** player on the **planet,** right?

SO WHAT MAKES MESSI SO FANTASTIC?

Movement
Small and quick – gets away from defenders.

Dribbling
No player keeps the ball at their feet better than Messi.

Passing
Always delivers the perfect ball to his team-mates.

Vision
He creates space and sees chances everywhere.

GOALS!
Of course, **Messi scores goals. LOADS** and **LOADS** and **LOADS** of **GOALS!**

Messi is simply **INCREDIBLE** all over the pitch.

HE IS THE ULTIMATE PLAYMAKER!

HOW AMAZING IS MESSI?

JUST LOOK AT THE NUMBERS . . .

5 . . . times winner of the Ballon d'Or

673 . . . total number of goals (so far)

10 . . . La Liga titles

68

... goals scored for Argentina

133 MILLION

... followers on Instagram

420

... goals scored in La Liga

An estimated

£99.8 MILLION

... earned in one year

MESSI I.D.

NAME:
Lionel Andrés Messi Cuccittini

NICKNAME:
The Flea

DATE OF BIRTH:
24 June 1987

PLACE OF BIRTH: *Rosario, Argentina*

HEIGHT: *1.70 m*

POSITION: *Forward*

CLUBS: *Newell's Old Boys (youth team), Barcelona*

NATIONAL TEAM: *Argentina*

LEFT OR RIGHT-FOOTED: *Left*

CHAPTER 2

LITTLE LEO

13

Lionel Messi was born in a town called Rosario in **ARGENTINA** in **1987.** All of his family loved playing and watching football, so Messi did, too!

Just as soon as he could walk, Messi would play football in the park with his brothers and cousins. They were all **older,** and much **BIGGER** than he was, but Lionel soon became the best player on the pitch.

They called him 'TITCH' because he was so small, but Messi didn't mind. It made him want to **play harder** and **become even better.**

When he was just **five** Leo joined his first club, ***GRANDOLI.*** His brothers Rodrigo and Matías played there, and his **grandmother** Celia took him to training.

Messi was already brilliant at ***PASSING, DRIBBLING*** and ***SCORING*** goals and the coach at Grandoli was amazed.

WOW, THIS BOY IS INCREDIBLE!

Leo trained really hard and his grandmother was always there, **CHEERING HIM ON.**

Leo was the **smallest** kid at school but
he was the **best footballer** by far.
When they played football at breaktime,
NOBODY COULD GET NEAR HIM!

Soon, the **whole town** of Rosario had heard about the **amazing little kid** who played for Grandoli. Lots of people would come and watch Messi's amazing skills.

It was **Messi's dream** to play for his local team,

NEWELL'S OLD BOYS.

His dream came true when he was just **six.**

20

At first, Messi played a **seven-a-side** game called **Baby Football**. In his first game for Newell's, he scored ***FOUR GOALS*** in a 6-0 win.

Messi's team were so good, nobody beat them for **three** years. They were known as

THE MACHINE OF '87

because that was the year most of the players were born.

Why is Messi like a baby?

Because he's good at dribbling!

One time, Messi was missing for the start of a game. When he finally turned up at half-time, the team were losing 1-0. Leo had been stuck **stuck in the toilet!**

Messi came on, *SCORED THREE GOALS* and Newell's won **3-1!**

Messi started playing **proper football** when he was **eleven.** With Messi, the team were so good, they beat other sides by as many as 15 goals. Some teams would stop the game after **NEWELL'S** scored six.

The **MACHINE OF '87** won everything - they were

UNSTOPPABLE!

In six years at Newell's, the young Messi scored over

500 GOALS.

Newell's Old Boys knew that Leo was very special. People said he was going to be a **LEGEND,** like the famous Argentine player

MARADONA.

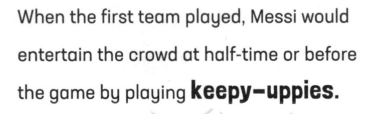

When the first team played, Messi would entertain the crowd at half-time or before the game by playing **keepy-uppies.**

ONE TIME HE DID 1,200!

Leo was very close to his grandmother. She had taken him to training at **Grandoli** and his first days at **Newell's.** She died when he was 10 and Leo was very upset.

Leo celebrated his first goal after she died by pointing both fingers to the sky.

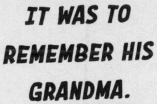

IT WAS TO REMEMBER HIS GRANDMA.

CHAPTER 4

BARCELONA BOUND

When Messi was 10, he started taking **medicine** to help him grow **taller,** but the medicine was very **expensive.** If he was going to be a top player, Leo and his family had to find a club that would pay for it.

ARGENTINA

That club was thousands of miles away in Spain.

SPAIN

BARCELONA

MESSI WAS GOING TO JOIN BARCELONA.

Leo signed for **BARCELONA** when he was just **13.** The club had never signed such a **young** player from so far away before. And he was so **small!**

The **bosses** were not sure about Messi at first. His **contract** was written out on a **napkin** in a restaurant!

But soon, they saw he was a **very, very special footballer.**

I always use a napkin when I'm eating!

Why?

Because I'm a **Messi** eater!

35

Leo's dad came to live with him in **Barcelona**, but he **missed his friends** and the rest of his family.

Then **Messi made two new friends,** defender **GERARD PIQUÉ**

GERARD PIQUÉ

CESC FÀBREGAS

and midfielder **CESC FÀBREGAS.** Leo was **much, much happier.** They gave Leo his nickname: **THE FLEA.**

Why do they call him 'The Flea'?

Because he is small, fast and a constant menace!

SCRATCH!
SCRATCH!

SCRATCH!
SCRATCH!

After training, the three boys would spend hours playing **PLAYSTATION** together.

Leo was the best, of course!

Messi, Piqué and **Fàbregas**

were part of the

GENERATION OF '87,

or the

BABY DREAM TEAM.

In the 2002-2003 season, they won the league and the Spanish and Catalan Cups. They were **UNBEATEN** all season and Messi scored **36 GOALS** in **30 GAMES.**

INCREDIBLE!

Leo began the 2003 Catalan Cup Final **wearing a face mask** because of an injury. He couldn't play in it, so he took it off. Then he **scored twice** in **10 minutes!**

That game became known as

THE GAME OF THE MASK.

CHAPTER 5

GOLDEN GOALS

GOAL #1

18 APRIL 2007
COPA DEL REY SEMI-FINAL, FIRST LEG

Barcelona 5-2 Getafe

Messi picked up the ball *IN HIS OWN HALF* and then got past two players.

Running at speed with the ball at his feet, Messi **zipped and turned** his way through **three** more opponents . . .

. . . before **dribbling** past the keeper and scoring.

THWACK!

AN AMAZING SOLO GOAL!

Barcelona's fans voted this the *best ever Barcelona goal.*

GOAL #2

30 MAY 2015
COPA DEL REY FINAL
Athletic Bilbao 1-3 Barcelona

Another **SUPERB SOLO** effort from Messi. He took the ball on the right, near the touchline.

He nipped past **one** . . .

two . . .

three . . .

players and was in the box.

He passed one more player and took a shot –

GOALLLLL!

What's the **second-best** Barcelona goal?

This one.

GOAL #3

27 APRIL 2011
CHAMPIONS LEAGUE SEMI-FINAL, FIRST LEG

Real Madrid 0-2 Barcelona

46

BOFFFF!

Playing against Barcelona's great rivals **REAL MADRID** in a massive Champions League game, Messi again made a solo run, **straight down the middle** with the ball.

He got past a Madrid defence that included *SERGIO RAMOS* to score his **second goal of the match.**

GENiUS!

Yep, this is the fans' *third-best* Barcelona goal!

"IS MESSI A REAL PLAYER OR A PLAYSTATION CHARACTER?"

Colombia striker Radamel Falcao

CHAPTER 6

THE BARÇA BROS

Messi played in **LA LIGA** for the first time in **2004.** Barcelona's superstar striker at the time was the Brazilian, **Ronaldinho.** He called Leo his **'LITTLE BROTHER'** and they became good friends.

Ronaldinho set up Messi's first Barcelona goal against Albacete in 2005. From then on, the two of them, along with **Samuel Eto'o** made a ***GREAT ATTACKING TRIO.***

RONALDINHO
2003-2008

250
APPEARANCES

110
GOALS

SAMUEL ETO'O *2004-2009*

234
APPEARANCES

152
GOALS

THIERRY HENRY *2007-2010*

121
APPEARANCES

49
GOALS

53

From **2004 TO 2015,** Messi played with the Spanish star midfielders **Xavi Hernández** and **Andrés Iniesta.**

Manager **Pep Guardiola** taught them to move and pass quickly, but keep possession.

They called it *TIKI-TAKA.*

IT WORKED!

With **Xavi** and **Iniesta**, Messi won *LA LIGA* seven times, the *COPA DEL REY* three times and the *CHAMPIONS LEAGUE* four times.

In the three seasons from 2014 to 2017, Barcelona had the amazing attacking trio of **MESSI, LUIS SUÁREZ** and **NEYMAR**. They were known as **MSN.**

Together, **MSN** were **UNSTOPPABLE.**

In their first season playing together, Barcelona won the **TREBLE** of **La Liga, the Copa del Rey** and **the Champions League.**

In total, they scored **364 GOALS** and recorded **211 ASSISTS.**

"IT WAS AN HONOUR TO BE THE COACH OF THE BEST PLAYER I HAVE EVER SEEN AND PROBABLY THE BEST I WILL SEE."
Pep Guardiola

CHAPTER 7

CHAMPIONS LEAGUE CHAMP

Messi's record in the **Champions League** is just incredible. Barcelona have won it *FOUR* times with Messi.

17 MAY 2006
STADE DE FRANCE, SAINT-DENIS, FRANCE
Barcelona 2-1 Arsenal

Messi didn't actually play in the final.

27 MAY 2009
STADIO OLIMPICO, ROME
Barcelona 2-0 Manchester United

28 MAY 2011
WEMBLEY STADIUM, LONDON

Barcelona 3-1 Manchester United

6 JUNE 2015
OLIMPIASTADION, BERLIN

Juventus 1-3 Barcelona

CHAMPIONS LEAGUE STAR

TOP CHAMPIONS LEAGUE SCORER

2008–09
9 goals

2009–10
8 goals

2010–11
12 goals

2011–12
14 goals

2014–15
10 goals

2018–19
12 goals

FASTEST PLAYER TO 100 CHAMPIONS LEAGUE GOALS

123 games

MOST CHAMPIONS LEAGUE GROUP STAGE GOALS

66 goals

CHAMPIONS LEAGUE HIGHLIGHTS

27 MAY 2009
FINAL

Barcelona 2-0 Manchester United

*Messi's awesome headed goal helped secure the title – and the **TREBLE** – for Barcelona.*

6 APRIL 2010
QUARTER-FINAL SECOND LEG

Barcelona 4-1 Arsenal *(6-3)*

*Trailing 1-0 after 19 minutes, Messi hit back with one, two, three, **FOUR** goals. Amazing!*

7 MARCH 2012
LAST-16 SECOND LEG

Barcelona 7-1 Bayer Leverkusen *(10-2)*

Messi scored an incredible **FIVE** *goals as Barça thrashed the German side.*

1 MAY 2019
SEMI-FINAL FIRST LEG

Barcelona 3-0 Liverpool

Messi's stunning free-kick was his second goal of the match – and his 600th for Barcelona.

HAT-TRICK HERO

You already know that Messi can score **FOUR** and **FIVE GOALS** in a single Champions League game. Here are some games where he only scored three.

Only three!

18 SEPTEMBER 2013
GROUP STAGE

Barcelona 4-0 Ajax

Messi's incredible trio of goals against Ajax included an awesome free-kick.

Ronaldo had scored a Champions League hat-trick the day before this one.

19 OCTOBER 2016
GROUP STAGE

Barcelona 4-0 Manchester City

Pep Guardiola was now City's manager and Messi reminded his old boss how good he was with a thrilling triple.

18 SEPTEMBER 2018
GROUP STAGE

Barcelona 4-0 PSV Eindhoven

Another Dutch team, another amazing free-kick and another hat-trick. Messi's 48th of his career.

BAYERN BRACE

This was a tough fixture. **Messi, Suárez, Neymar** and their team-mates faced a strong Bayern side led by former Barça boss **Pep Guardiola.**

BOATENG

It was **0-0** all the way until the 77th minute, when Messi fired in a low, deadly shot. **1-0!**

Just three minutes later, Messi scored again. He turned past defender **Jerome Boateng,** who fell to the floor, and chipped the ball over the head of Bayern keeper **Manu Neuer. 2-0!**

THAT'S GENIUS!

NEUER

Then **Neymar** made it **3-0** and Bayern were finished.

IT WAS ONE OF MESSI'S BEST PERFORMANCES.

After the game, the Barcelona manager **Luis Enrique** said:

"WITH MESSI, FOOTBALL IS EASIER. HE'S A PLAYER FROM ANOTHER DIMENSION. AND WE CAN ENJOY HIM EVERY DAY."

CHAPTER 8

DOUBLES AND TREBLES

71

When Ronaldinho left Barcelona in 2008, Messi took the famous **number 10** shirt. **Messi** played with **Xavi** and **Iniesta** in midfield, and **Samuel Eto'o** and **Thierry Henry** up front.

The team played brilliantly together. One time, they beat Real Madrid - away - **6-2.**

IT WAS A SPECIAL TEAM FOR A SPECIAL SEASON . . .

TREBLE 2008-09

Barcelona beat **Athletic Bilbao 4-1** to win the **Copa del Rey...**

...finished **nine points** ahead of **Real Madrid** to win **La Liga ...**

...and beat **Manchester United 2-0** to win the **Champions League.**

Messi scored **38 goals** that season.
Added to **Eto'o** and **Henry's** tally, it was
100 GOALS.

Barcelona and Messi had made **HISTORY.** It was the **first time** that any Spanish team had won a **TREBLE.**

They also won the **Supercopa de España**, the **UEFA Super Cup** and the **FIFA Club World Cup**.

That's an incredible **SIX TROPHIES IN ONE YEAR.**

No other team has done that. *Ever!*

TREBLE

Incredibly, **six years later,**
BARCELONA DID IT AGAIN!

It was Messi's **first season**

playing with **Suárez** and **Neymar.**

MSN SCORED 122 GOALS!

They beat **Athletic Bilbao** again, this time **3–1**, to win **Copa del Rey**.

Real Madrid were just **two points** behind when they won **La Liga**.

The **Champions League** was sealed with a **3–1** win over **Juventus**.

They were the first team to win a *treble*, twice!

Is two **TREBLES** enough for Messi? **No way!**

He has also helped Barcelona win three

DOUBLES!

2010-11
La Liga
Champions League

2015-16
La Liga
Copa del Rey

2017-18
La Liga
Copa del Rey

CHAPTER 9

ARGENTINE ICON

In 2005, when he was 18,

Leo played for Argentina at the

FIFA World Youth Championship.

Pablo Zabaleta

was the

captain and . . .

. . . **Sergio Agüero** was in

the squad, too.

Messi scored both goals when **Argentina** beat **Nigeria** 2=1 in the final. He was a

WORLD CHAMPION!

Aguero has been Leo's **best friend** ever since this tournament.

OLYMPIC MEDAL WINNER, BEIJING 2008

Messi teamed up with Zabaleta and Agüero again for the **2008 OLYMPIC GAMES** in Beijing. **Ángel di María** was also in the team.

They beat **Brazil 3-0** in the semi-final and **Nigeria 1-0** in the final to win . . .

OLYMPIC GOLD.

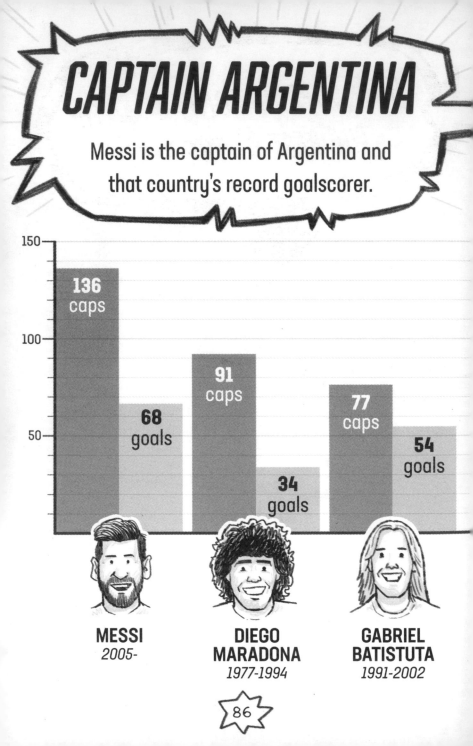

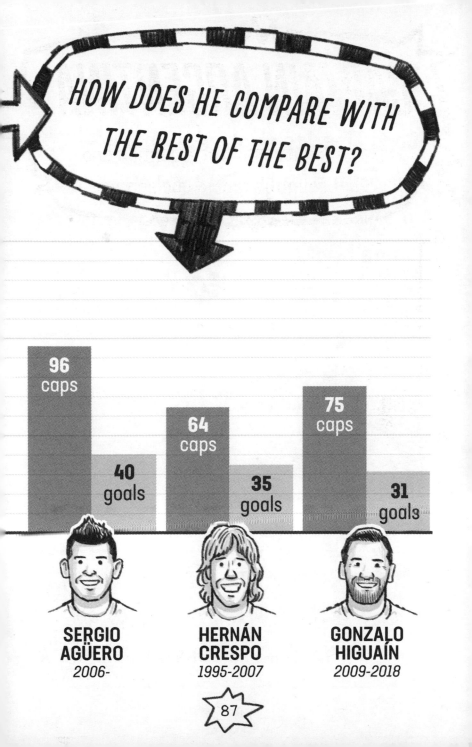

In **2016**, after losing to **Chile** in the **Copa America final,** Messi retired from international football. But the whole country, including the **president,** asked him to **come back!**

SO HE DID.

DON'T GO, LEO!

"I GAVE SERIOUS THOUGHT TO QUITTING, BUT MY LOVE FOR MY COUNTRY AND THIS SHIRT IS TOO GREAT."

CHAPTER 10

LA LIGA LIFE

LA LIGA GOAL MACHINE

In 15 seasons, Messi has scored more than **400 goals** for Barcelona in La Liga.

Nobody has **scored more** La Liga **goals** than **Messi**. **EVER.**

SEASON	APPEARANCES	GOALS
2004-05	7	1
2005-06	17	6
2006-07	26	14
2007-08	28	10
2008-09	31	23
2009-10	35	34
2010-11	33	31
2011-12	37	50
2012-13	32	46
2013-14	31	28
2014-15	38	43
2015-16	33	26
2016-17	34	37
2017-18	36	34
2018-19	34	36
TOTAL	452	419

Messi's record in La Liga is

UNBELIEVABLE.

LA LIGA TOP SCORER

2009-10
34 GOALS

2011-12
50 GOALS

2012-13
46 GOALS

2016-17
37 GOALS

2017-18
34 GOALS

2018-19
36 GOALS

50 GOALS IN LA LIGA 2011-12

The **most goals ever scored** by a player **in one season** in La Liga.

33 LA LIGA HAT-TRICKS

A record for Barcelona.

HAT-TRICK HERO

Messi has scored an incredible **33 hat-tricks** in **La Liga.** These are some of his best.

10 MARCH 2007
Barcelona 3-3 Real Madrid

Messi's first hat-trick for Barcelona was against their great rivals Real Madrid. Wow!

19 FEBRUARY 2012
Barcelona 5-1 Valencia

*Messi scored **FOUR** of five Barca goals. One of **FOUR** hat-tricks for Messi against Valencia.*

23 FEBRUARY 2019
Sevilla 2-4 Barcelona

*Away at Sevilla, Messi scored three brilliant goals to record the **50th** hat-trick of his career.*

EL CLÁSICO CLASSICS

Barcelona versus **Real Madrid** is one of the biggest games in world football. It's called

EL CLÀSICO.

2 MAY 2009
Real Madrid 2-6 Barcelona

Messi scored two and his old friend Gerard Piqué got the sixth goal as Madrid were hammered at home.

29 NOVEMBER 2010
Barcelona 5-0 Real Madrid

No goals from Messi, but two assists helped deliver this thumping. It was Madrid manager Jose Mourinho's first El Clásico.

23 MARCH 2014
Real Madrid 3-4 Barcelona

A Ronaldo penalty, Sergio Ramos sent off and two Messi penalties to complete his hat-trick. A thriller of a game!

23 APRIL 2017
Real Madrid 2-Barcelona 3

Messi's injury-time goal finished this end-of-season monster El Clásico. It was his 500th goal for Barcelona and he celebrated by holding up his shirt for the Barça fans. **Nice.**

He got a yellow card for doing this!

CHAPTER 11

MESSI VS RONALDO

99

The Ballon d'Or (The Golden Ball)

is a **PRIZE** awarded to the **best footballer** each year.

LOOK AT THE RESULTS SINCE RONALDO WON IT FIRST.

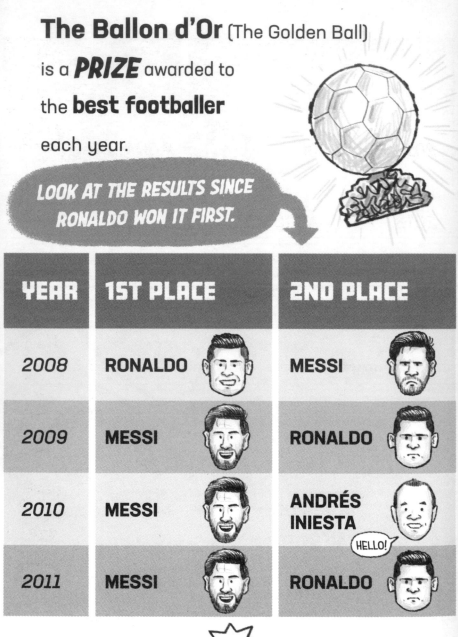

YEAR	1ST PLACE	2ND PLACE
2008	RONALDO	MESSI
2009	MESSI	RONALDO
2010	MESSI	ANDRÉS INIESTA *HELLO!*
2011	MESSI	RONALDO

YEAR	1ST PLACE	2ND PLACE
2012	MESSI	RONALDO
2013	RONALDO	MESSI
2014	RONALDO	MESSI
2015	MESSI	RONALDO
2016	RONALDO	MESSI
2017	RONALDO	MESSI
2018	LUKA MODRIĆ	RONALDO

GRRR!

INTERNATIONAL PENALTIES SCORED
14   9

CHAMPIONS LEAGUE MEDALS
4   5

CHAMPIONS LEAGUE GOALS
112   128

WORLD CUP GOALS
6   7

LEAGUE TITLES
10   6

MAJOR CUP TITLES
17   12

GOLDEN SHOE WINS
6   4

MESSI vs RONALDO
IN LA LIGA

SEASON	MESSI GOALS	RONALDO GOALS
2009–10	34	26
2010–11	31	40
2011–12	50	46
2012–13	46	34
2013–14	28	31
2014–15	43	48
2015–16	26	35
2016–17	37	25
2017–18	34	26
TOTAL	329	311

SUPER FLEA

Messi is one of the fastest players

in the world - he's recorded a speed of

32.5 KM/H!

He's not THE fastest player, but **nobody dribbles** the **ball at speed like Messi.**

109

FANTASTIC FEINTS

The **BODY FEINT** is where a player tricks his opponent into thinking he's **GOING ONE WAY . . .**

. . . THEN GOES THE OTHER.

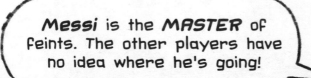

Messi is the **MASTER** of feints. The other players have no idea where he's going!

111

NUTMEG
MASTER

The **NUTMEG** is a trick where a player moves the ball between his opponent's legs.

NIGEL NUTMEG, AN ACTUAL NUTMEG!

NUTMEGS RULE!

Messi is **SUPERB** at nutmegs. Sometimes he passes to a team-mate, but when Messi picks the ball up again and continues his run, it's *EXTRA-SPECIAL.*

SOMETIMES, A MESSI NUTMEG LEAVES A PLAYER ON THE FLOOR!

"WHAT LEO DOES IS SO INCREDIBLE THAT I HAVE TO BE CAREFUL NOT TO STAND STILL WATCHING HIM MAKE HIS MOVES."

Thierry Henry , when he played alongside Messi

114

CHAPTER 13

THE G.O.A.T.

(GREATEST OF ALL TIME)

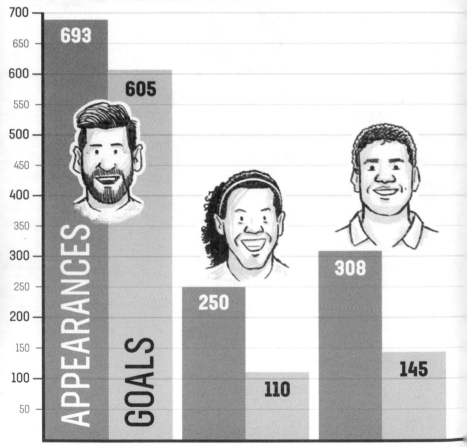

MANY INCREDIBLE STRIKERS HAVE PLAYED FOR BARCELONA.

APPEARANCES **GOALS**

MESSI
2004-
693 / 605

RONALDINHO
2003-2008
250 / 110

PATRICK KLUIVERT
1998-2004
308 / 145

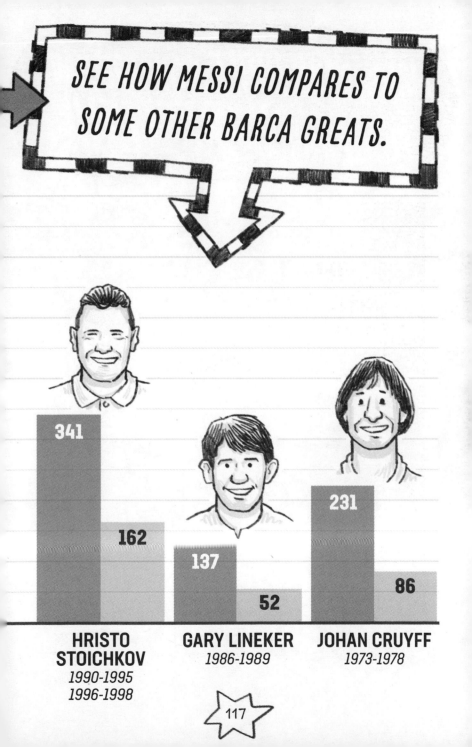

SEE HOW MESSI COMPARES TO SOME OTHER BARCA GREATS.

341

162

137

52

231

86

HRISTO STOICHKOV
1990-1995
1996-1998

GARY LINEKER
1986-1989

JOHAN CRUYFF
1973-1978

How much would it cost to buy Messi?

ABOUT . . .

£135 MILLION!

What else could you buy with all that cash?

135 *McLaren P1 supercars*

ONE *billionaire's superyacht*
(including a helicopter and a speedboat)

MESSI RECORDS

(YOU MIGHT NOT KNOW)

Most goals scored in a calendar year: 91 (2012)

Shared highest scorer in a UEFA Champions League game: 5

Youngest player to win 5 Ballon d'Or awards.

Most goals scored in La Liga El Clásico matches: 18

Most league goals in history across Europe's top 5 leagues: 421

Only player to score in 23 different cities in the Champions League.

Youngest player to reach 100 Champions League appearances.

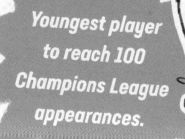

Most assists in La Liga: 170

Most free kicks scored for Barcelona: 43

LEGENDS

Messi will go down in history as one of the **giants of football.**

MESSI
2004-

PELÉ
Three-times
World Cup winner
1956-1977

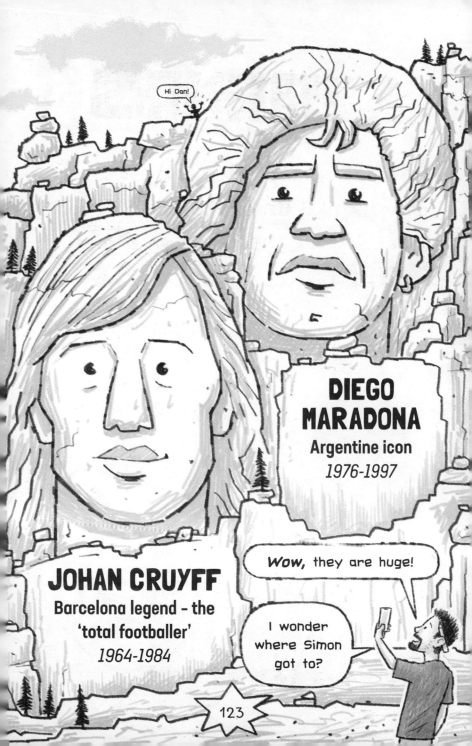

QUIZ TIME!

How much do you know about Messi? Try this quiz to find out, then test your friends!

1. How many times has Messi won La Liga?

----

2. Which team did he play for before Barcelona?

----

3. Name the two other players in 'MSN'?

----

4. Who called Leo his 'Little Brother'?

----

5. In which year did he win his first Ballon d'Or?

----

6. In which year did Messi win an Olympic Gold Medal?

----

7. How many goals did he score in La Liga in 2011-12?

----

8. In which season did Messi win the Treble with Barcelona for the second time?

----

9. Who is Messi's biggest rival in football?

----

10. Messi scored his 500th goal against which team in 2017?

The answers are on the next page. *But no peeking!*

ANSWERS

1. 10

2. Newell's Old Boys

3. Luis Suárez, Neymar

4. Ronaldinho

5. 2009

6. 2008

7. 50

8. 2014-2015

9. Cristiano Ronaldo

10. Real Madrid

MESSI:
WORDS YOU NEED TO KNOW

Ballon d'Or
Award given to the male player who has played the best over a year. Awarded each December by *France Football* magazine.

Copa Del Rey
Spanish knockout cup competition.

FIFA Club World Cup
Knockout cup competition between clubs from around the world.

La Liga
The top football league in Spain.

El Clásico
The match between Barcelona and Real Madrid.

UEFA Champions League
European club competition held every year. The winner is the best team in Europe.

Supercopa de España
Match played between the La Liga champions and the winners of the Copa Del Rey.

ABOUT THE AUTHORS

Simon's first job was at the Science Museum, making paper aeroplanes and blowing bubbles big enough for your dad to stand in. Since then he's written all sorts of books about the stuff he likes, from dinosaurs and rockets, to llamas, loud music and of course, football. Simon has supported Ipswich Town since they won the FA Cup in 1978 (it's true - look it up) and once sat next to Rio Ferdinand on a train. He lives in Kent with his wife and daughter, two tortoises and a cat.

Dan has drawn silly pictures since he could hold a crayon. Then he grew up and started making books about stuff like trucks, space, people's jobs, *Doctor Who* and *Star Wars*. Dan remembers Ipswich Town winning the FA cup but he didn't watch it because he was too busy making a Viking ship out of brown paper. As a result, he knows more about Vikings than football. Dan lives in Suffolk with his wife, son, daughter and a dog that takes him for very long walks.